The Heart of
Burgundy

Other Books by Andy Katz

———

A PORTRAIT OF
NAPA AND SONOMA

VINEYARD: A YEAR IN THE
LIFE OF CALIFORNIA'S
WINE COUNTRY

The Heart of

Burgundy

A PORTRAIT OF THE
FRENCH COUNTRYSIDE
BY
Andy Katz

INTRODUCTION BY ROBERT M. PARKER, JR.

SIMON & SCHUSTER

To my son, Jesse,
with all my love

SIMON & SCHUSTER
Rockefeller Center
1230 Avenue of the Americas
New York, NY 10020

SIMON & SCHUSTER and colophon
are registered trademarks of Simon & Schuster, Inc.

Designed by Joel Avirom, Meghan Day Healey,
and Jason Snyder

Manufactured in Italy

10 9 8 7 6 5 4 3 2 1

Library of Congress Cataloging-in-Publication Data
Katz, Andy, date.
    The heart of Burgundy : a portrait of the French
countryside / by Andy Katz ; introduction by
Robert M. Parker, Jr.
        p.   cm.
    1. Wine and winemaking—France—Burgundy
Pictorial Works. I. Title.
TP553.K38   1999
641.2'2'09444—dc21   99-32165
                                CIP

ISBN 0-684-84595-4

ACKNOWLEDGMENTS

To the people who made my life in Burgundy a total joy: Olivier Leflaive, Anne-Claude Leflaive, André and Ann Ropiteau, Pascal Wagner, Philippe Senard, François Faively, Serge and Karen Demolliere, René Tosett and Françoise Lequin, Charles Rousseau, Jacques Seysses, François Labet, Jacques Lardière, and Nicolas Potel. Without their help, this would have been a lot more difficult and, more important, with whom would I have shared their brilliant wine?

I would also like to thank the many people who helped me with this project, and specifically Joel Avirom, Janice Easton, Dan Green, Robert Parker, Kathy Katz, Larry Katz, Roger Bohmrich, and Michael Ditch.

Much appreciation for the people who bought my portfolio, which allowed me to pursue this project: Tom Arnold, Henry and Ann Beer, Howard and Terry Bittman, Joe and Marilyn Davis, Fred Drake, Charles Durrell, Howard and Irene Levine, Chuck and Elizabeth Meyers, Court Newberry, Ed and Beth Parent, Tim and Linda Stancliff, Bruce and Stephanie Westhusin, Travis and Sue Ellen White, and Peter and Michelle Wise.

INTRODUCTION BY ROBERT M. PARKER, JR.

While Andy Katz's exquisite photographs of Burgundy easily stand on their own, it really isn't appropriate to look at them without a brief understanding of the unique qualities of this area. The Burgundy area of eastern France encompasses five basic regions: Chablis, Côte d'Or (which contains the two famous golden slopes called the Côte de Beaune and Côte de Nuits), Côte Chalonnaise, Mâconnais, and Beaujolais. Unlike Bordeaux, which is bounded on one side by the ocean and on the other by the Gironde River, Burgundy has no major bodies of water to affect its climate and consequently is shaped significantly by the west winds that buffet it, along with the significant rainfall and devastating hailstorms they often carry. While this can be a detriment to the wine producers of the region, Burgundy's northerly latitude also provides for longer hours of daylight during the important summer growing months, so with dry, sunny weather from the beginning of September onward, a fine crop can still be produced.

The majority of the region's soil is made up of kimmeridge clay and limestone. In Chablis, this soil and its cousin, the portlandian limestone, are ideal for Chardonnay grapes. The famed Côte d'Or, which for many connoisseurs of Burgundy is that region's beginning and end, is essentially a limestone ridge representing the eastern edge of a calcareous plateau that empties into the Saône River basin. The northern half, the Côte de Nuits, has an easterly orientation that gradually shifts toward a more southeasterly exposure. This ridge runs for about thirty-one miles between Marsannay and Santenay. In the Côte Chalonnaise, the limestone ridge begins to break up into a chain of small hills that have limestone subsoils with clay/sand topsoils that are occasionally enriched with iron deposits. However, the underlying limestone strata are still present and continue not only through the Côte Chalonnaise, but also through the pastoral, rolling hills of the neighboring Mâconnais region, giving way finally to the granite-based soils of the Beaujolais region.

Geologists believe the limestone shelf now called the Côte d'Or was formed over 150 million years ago, well before man appeared on the scene. During what is called the Jurassic period (between 135 and 195 million years ago), the geological face of Burgundy began to take shape. Formed during this epoch were the petrified remains of sea life, compressed over time with a calcareous mudstone, as well as the rock that resulted from the precipitation of lime from the seawater that then covered Burgundy. The limestone rocks sprinkled with marlstone constitute the backbone of the various hillsides and most renowned vineyard sites of not only the Côte d'Or, but also the slopes of Chablis, the Côte Chalonnaise, and the Mâconnais.

The climate and the soil are two of the distinct features of Burgundy; the people and their culture are another. Viticulture is believed to have been launched in Burgundy by either the Greeks or the Romans. There was a thriving Greek settlement at Marseilles around 600 B.C., leading some observers to surmise that the Greeks traveling through the Rhône Valley were responsible for the vineyards planted along the hillsides of the Rhône River as well as those farther north in Burgundy. Other observers claim that viticulture was brought to Burgundy by the Romans, whose influence can be seen in the architectural ruins that archae-ologists have unearthed. With Caesar's conquest of Gaul in 52 B.C. came a degree of stability and civilization that provided the necessary economy to foster the production of wine, and it would be unlikely that the wine-loving Romans would not have encouraged vineyard development and wine production in the territory. However, the absence of any hard evidence makes such theories conjectural.

Burgundy came into its own during the Middle Ages, with the flourishing of the Catholic Church, and more specifically under the Benedictine order of Cluny. In A.D. 1098 a Benedictine order, the Cistercians, was established at the Abbey of Cîteaux in a desolate area just to the east of the village of Nuits St.-Georges. These monks were renowned for their religious enthusiasm, work ethic, spartan lifestyle, and adherence to physically exhausting hard labor. This philosophy apparently led to the Cistercians' decision to cultivate the poor, infertile, rocky soil of what today is known as the Côte d'Or. This stretch of limestone hillsides had long proved unsuitable for crops, but the Cistercians, with their commitment to backbreaking labor, believed the vine could be cultivated and quality wine produced.

The expansion and empire building of the ecclesiastic orders in Burgundy was impressive, even by today's standards. In A.D. 1141 the nuns of the Cistercian Abbey of Notre Dame du Tart purchased a vineyard in Morey St.-Denis that became known as the Clos de Tart. It remained under their control until the French Revolution. The Cistercians also launched a branch of their order at the Clos de Vougeot, which hundreds of years later became part of the elaborate appellation system imposed on all of the best winemaking regions of France. Ultimately the religious orders controlled much of the wine that was shipped to the government in Paris, principally because France's other renowned viticultural region, Bordeaux, was at that time controlled by the English and their desire for claret.

The height of Burgundy's power, historically referred to as the Golden Age, ranged from the middle of the fourteenth century to the middle of the fifteenth century. During this era the great dukes of Burgundy controlled not only Burgundy, but also the majority of northern France and large portions of what is now Belgium, the Netherlands, and Luxembourg. This period witnessed an extraordinary flourishing of art, architecture, and music. Under the dukes, the huge monastic orders prospered even further. They were the beneficiaries of large land grants and were encouraged by the dukes to build great abbeys and cathedrals. To no one's surprise, the church's chief worldly export, wine, prospered as well.

The French Revolution of 1789 fundamentally altered the landscape of Burgundy, tearing apart most of the gigantic wine estates owned by the wealthy and the monastic orders. Subsequently, the Napoleonic-Sallic Code increased the fragmentation of Burgundy's vineyards. This code required that upon the death of a parent the land be divided equally among all sons. With each new generation Burgundy's lands became more and more fragmented, each parcel owned by a different person. Today's Burgundy is, therefore, distressingly difficult to grasp and comprehend. This multiple ownership of the same vineyard reaches its preposterous, dizzyingly frustrating absurdity with the great vineyard of Clos Vougeot, which possesses 124 acres and seventy-seven-plus landowners. One hardly needs to be reminded of the infinite number of variations in quality that can occur from the same vineyard when the wine is made by as many as six dozen different producers.

In the late nineteenth century Burgundy was ravaged by the phylloxera epidemic that devastated all of Europe's vineyards. While Burgundy did escape serious damage during World War I, the area was occupied by Germany during World War II. In late 1944

and early 1945 there were some small but fierce battles between the Allied forces and the retreating Germans, particularly in the Côte de Beaune. An endearing story of a French commander has emerged from the skirmishes of the last years of World War II. The commander apparently delayed his attack on the retreating Germans for fear of damaging the best Premier Cru and Grand Cru vineyards of Chassagne-Montrachet, Puligny-Montrachet, and Meursault. When he was subsequently apprised the Germans were occupying the lower slopes, or those vineyards not entitled to Premier Cru or Grand Cru status, he immediately ordered his soldiers to attack the German positions.

This is the rich history that comes to mind when I view Andy Katz's photos, and I wonder about the timelessness of nature. While the vines and people may have changed over the centuries, the soil and the method of cultivating grapes to wine really hasn't. The walls that border the vineyard may be only five hundred years old, but the rocks they contain remember dinosaurs and other creatures of which we can only dream. And that little shady spot where the oak bows over the wall looks like the perfect place to sit, drink a glass of Beaujolais, and contemplate it all. Please enjoy these incomparable photos, which brought new meaning to me, of a region I know and love.

PREFACE BY ANDY KATZ

*T*he Côte d'Or just days ago was a sea of gold varying in shade depending on the sun's angle. Today, the gold I see lies in the most important natural resource in Burgundy—the soil.

If you ask the most famous winemakers in Burgundy the reason their wine is among the most sought-after in the world, you may be surprised at the answer. The care with which the grapes are harvested? The intensity of the rain, or the warmth of the sun? The talents of the vintner? No, the answer is always the same. It's the unique qualities of the terrain, its dense, rocky soil.

There is a modesty and grace in that answer which humbles me. These people are as connected to their land as the roots of the vines they tend. While I have captured mere minutes of their beauty to bring home and reproduce, they will continue to enjoy their seasons of harvest and rest. My project has come to an end, and I'm sad to leave my wonderful house beside a vineyard in the great village of Monthélie. I'll miss tramping around the countryside in search of that

elusive light I crave, but most of all I'll miss the smiles and the enthusiasm of the people,
whose passion for winemaking and life is contagious.

While I take photos of many different subjects, this is my third book of photos in vineyards. What attracts me to wine regions, other than the obvious taste for the grape, is the
people. Throughout the world, people in wine country have a certain remarkable enthusiasm—a true passion for winemaking: "Ah, 1990, now that was a year, '95 is tasting wonderful,
and the '96 could be something special . . ."

Is my project complete? The question tortures me as I contemplate leaving any great
site, but I can never hope to fully capture any location. I could live my entire life here and still
miss some brilliant images. I have greeted the sun here every morning, and have said *bonne
nuit* to it every night. The skies have been magnificent, and I must be content.

So I must end it here, and thank all my friends, my gracious hosts, and all the people
who said, "*Bonjour, Monsieur.*"

23

44

52

88

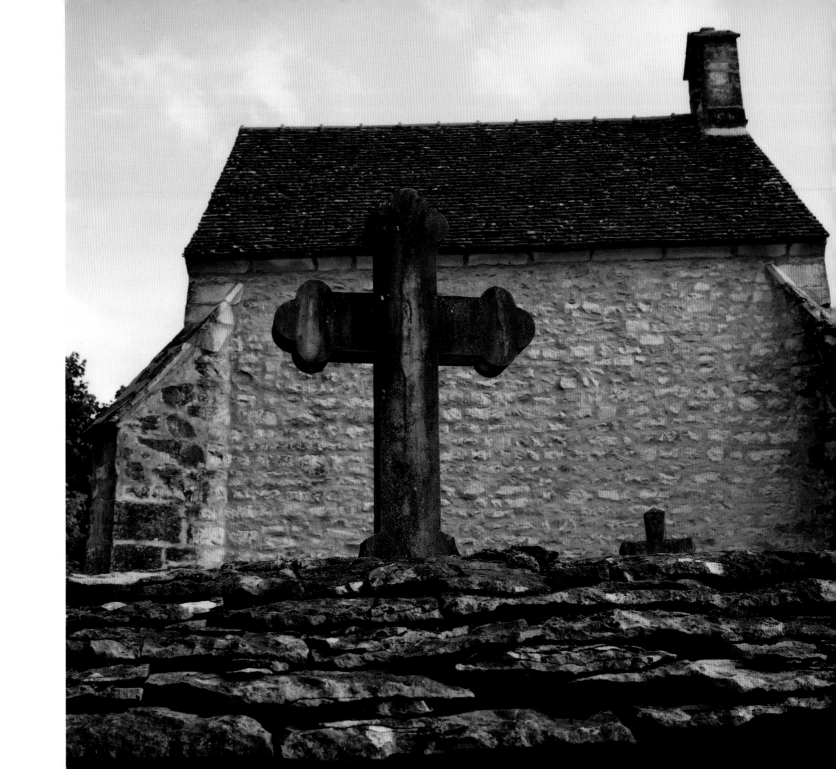

PHOTOGRAPHIC NOTES

While having a job that entails living on a vineyard, drinking fine wines, and spending days on end with wonderfully hospitable people is in many ways ideal, there is one major drawback. Because the beauty of the light is one of the most important details in my work, I have to be up before the sun every day.

Every day starts the same way, with an awful buzz informing me that there is one hour before the sun will rise to greet me with its magnificent rays. This and only this is the bad part of my job. If I've been up before the sun for the last ten days in a row, I'll think to myself, "I could certainly sleep in today. Could it be cloudy? Could it please rain?" When the sun shines yet again—perfect weather I would otherwise be praying for—I think, "What could I possibly miss?" But each time I find the strength to haul myself out of bed yet again by remembering that this morning could be the best yet. Every day is a new opportunity.

After pulling up the jeans and strapping on the camera gear I'm up and out, traveling to a predesignated spot where I'll wait for the sun. There it is! I now have twenty minutes of gorgeous light and must use it well. It is amazing how quickly the light can turn from magnificent to harsh, a matter of minutes. I then pack it up and head back to my *gite*, that wonderful little house on the edge of the vineyard that is pictured on the cover. No longer regretting my early awakening, I think only how lucky I was to be blessed with the morning.

Now it's time to get on my bicycle and ride to Meursault, where my baguette and freshly brewed coffee await me in a local café. The rest of the day is spent scouting out areas for late afternoon light shots or next morning's sunrise photos. Because of all this location work, I try to keep my equipment simple. I shoot with a Mamiya 7 "RZ67" and for close-ups I've been using the Mamiya 645 with its incredible macro lens. I almost always use a tripod (so I can drink as much coffee as I want), and I shoot exclusively with color negative film, primarily Fuji N.P.H. I find color negative film to have tremendous advantages over transparency film. With the dramatic lighting I strive for, transparency film has a difficult time holding up highlight and shadow details simultaneously.

I print all my own work, usually when I'm home in Boulder, Colorado. The truth of the matter is that I absolutely love what I do, and I wouldn't give that pleasure over to anyone else. The satisfaction of producing images that are appealing on both an aesthetic and an emotional level is what I strive for. I hope this book communicates that. This is obviously for you, the reader, to decide.

Selected Photographic Locations